Entrepreneurial Traits

OG Arizechi

Published by KA Publishing Press Ltd, 2023.

Table of Contents

Entrepreneurial Traits -

Discover The 15 Traits of Successful Entrepreneurs

Introduction

Ever wondered if entrepreneurs are just born lucky, or if anyone can become a business whiz? It's a question that puzzles many when they dive into the wild world of starting and running a business. Turning a simple idea into a cash-churning business is no walk in the park.

Now, you might think being born rich gives you a head start. But let me tell you, hard work can outrun raw talent any day. That means you, yes, you, can become a successful entrepreneur if you're ready to roll up your sleeves and work smart. Do you think you've got what it takes to make it big?

Guess what? According to Entrepreneur.com, entrepreneurs aren't cut from the same cookie cutter. They come from different corners of the world, have diverse upbringings, education levels, and social backgrounds.

But hey, being an entrepreneur isn't just about luck or genes. It's about putting in the hustle and using your smarts. So, are you up for the challenge?

Picture this: You, working hard, making smart moves, and turning your idea into a booming business. It's not about where you start; it's about how far you're willing to go. Ready to dive in and discover how to make it happen? Let's get started!"

Crave Learning – Growth Mindset

Do you want to be a successful entrepreneur? If so, you need to love learning new things. The world is changing fast, and you need to keep up with it. You can't just do the same thing over and over and expect to succeed. You need to learn new skills, new ideas, and new ways of doing things.

Learning is not boring or hard. It's fun and easy if you know how to do it right. Here are some tips to help you learn more and better: -

Read books every day.

Books are like treasure chests of knowledge. They can teach you anything you want to know. You can learn from the best experts in any field. You can also learn from the stories and experiences of other entrepreneurs who have done what you want to do. Reading books will expand your mind and inspire you to take action.

Follow the news every day.

The news can tell you what's happening in your industry and in the world. You can learn about the latest trends, opportunities, and challenges. You can also learn from the successes and failures of other businesses. Following the news will keep you informed and alert.

Take courses online or offline.

Courses are like shortcuts to learning. They can teach you the most important and useful things in a short time. You can learn from the best teachers and coaches who have proven results. You can also interact with other students who have similar goals and interests. Taking courses will boost your skills and confidence.

Join masterminds or mentorship programs.

Masterminds and mentorship programs are like support groups for learning. They can help you connect with other entrepreneurs who are on the same journey as you. You can learn from their advice, feedback, and encouragement. You can also share your own insights, challenges, and achievements. Joining masterminds or mentorship programs will increase your motivation and accountability.

Watch YouTube videos and/or listen to podcasts.

YouTube videos and podcasts are like snacks for learning. They can teach you something new or interesting in a few minutes. You can learn from the most entertaining and engaging content creators who have millions of fans. You can also choose from a variety of topics and formats that suit your taste and mood. Watching YouTube videos or listening to podcasts will make learning fun and easy.

These are some of the ways you can learn more and better as an entrepreneur. But don't just learn for the sake of learning. Learn for the sake of doing. Apply what you learn to your own business and see what works and what doesn't. Experiment, test, and improve until you find the best solution for your problem.

———

One example of an entrepreneur who loves learning is **Elon Musk**. He is the founder of Tesla, SpaceX, Neuralink, and many other companies that are changing the world. He is also one of the richest people in the world. How did he become so successful? By learning constantly.

He learned how to build rockets by reading books. He learned how to run a car company by taking courses. He learned how to create a brain-computer interface by hiring experts. He learned how to make money by watching YouTube videos. He learned how to inspire people by listening to podcasts.

He didn't just learn these things for fun. He learned them for a purpose: to make his vision a reality. He applied what he learned to his own businesses and made them successful.

So, don't delay. Up your learning game today!

Visionary

Do you have a big dream for your business? Do you want to create something amazing that no one else has done before? If so, you need to be a visionary entrepreneur.

A visionary entrepreneur is someone who can see the future and make it happen. They can spot an opportunity and imagine reaching incredible heights that others can't. They can also lead the way in new fields and innovations.

Being a visionary entrepreneur is not easy. You will face many challenges and doubts along the way. You will have to deal with people who don't believe in you or your idea. You will have to overcome obstacles and risks that might seem impossible.

But being a visionary entrepreneur is also rewarding. You will be able to make a positive impact on the world and change it for the better. You will be able to achieve your goals and fulfill your potential. You will be able to enjoy the fruits of your hard work and creativity.

So how can you become a visionary entrepreneur? Here are some tips to help you: -

Find your passion.

Visionary entrepreneurs are passionate about what they do. They love their work, and they are driven by it. They don't do it for money or fame, but for a higher purpose. Find something that you are passionate about and that you can make a difference with.

Think big.

Visionary entrepreneurs think big and bold. They don't settle for small or average results. They aim for the stars and beyond. They have a clear vision of what they want to achieve and how they want to do it. Think big and don't limit yourself by what others think or say.

Learn constantly.

Visionary entrepreneurs learn constantly and never stop. They are curious and eager to learn new things. They read books, take courses, watch videos, listen to podcasts, join masterminds, seek mentorship, and do everything they can to learn more and better. They also learn from their own experiences, mistakes, and feedback. Learn constantly and keep improving yourself and your business.

Innovate constantly.

Visionary entrepreneurs innovate constantly and never stop. They are creative and original in their ideas and solutions. They don't copy or follow others, but they create their own path. They also adapt and evolve with the changing market and customer needs. Innovate constantly and keep offering value and uniqueness to your customers.

Take action.

Visionary entrepreneurs take action and never stop. They don't just dream or plan, but they do. They execute their vision with courage and determination. They don't let fear or doubt stop them, but they overcome them with action. They also test and measure their results and make adjustments as needed. Take action and make your vision a reality.

———

One example of a visionary entrepreneur is **Jeff Bezos**. He is the founder of Amazon, one of the largest and most successful companies in the world. He is also one of the richest people in the world.

How did he become so successful? By being a visionary entrepreneur.

He started Amazon in 1994 as an online bookstore. He saw an opportunity to sell books online when the internet was still new and growing. He imagined reaching millions of customers around the world with his online store.

But he didn't stop there. He expanded Amazon into selling other products, such as music, movies, electronics, clothing, toys, groceries, etc. He also created other services, such as Kindle, Prime, Alexa, AWS, etc. He also ventured into other industries, such as space exploration with Blue Origin and media with The Washington Post.

He did all this by following his passion for innovation and customer satisfaction. He thought big and bold about his vision and goals. He learned constantly from books, mentors, competitors, customers, etc. He innovated constantly by creating new products, services, features, etc. He took action by executing his plans with speed and efficiency.

So, what are you waiting for? Become a visionary entrepreneur today and change the world.

12

Risk Taker

Do you want to be a successful entrepreneur? If so, you need to be a risk taker. Risk takers are entrepreneurs who are willing to take chances and face uncertainty and failure. They are not afraid of trying new things and going after their goals. They are the ones who make headlines and change the world.

But being a risk taker does not mean being reckless or foolish. It means being smart and strategic. It means taking calculated risks that have a high potential for reward and a low potential for loss. It means having a plan and a backup plan in case things go wrong.

Here are some tips to help you become a risk taker: -

Know your strengths and weaknesses.

Risk takers know what they are good at and what they are not. They focus on their strengths and leverage them to their advantage. They also acknowledge their weaknesses and work on improving them or finding partners who can complement them. Knowing your strengths and weaknesses will help you assess your risks and opportunities better.

Do your research and analysis.

Risk takers do not jump into things blindly. They do their homework and gather as much information as possible. They analyze the market, the competition, the customer, the trends, the costs, the benefits, etc. They weigh the pros and cons of each option and scenario. Doing your research and analysis will help you make informed and rational decisions.

Trust your intuition and creativity.

Risk takers trust their gut feelings and their imagination. They listen to their inner voice and follow their instincts. They also use their creativity to come up with original and innovative ideas and solutions. They don't just copy or follow others, but they create their own path. Trusting your intuition and creativity will help you discover new possibilities and opportunities.

Take action and learn from feedback.

Risk takers take action and don't let fear or doubt stop them. They execute their plans with courage and determination. They also learn from their feedback, whether positive or negative. They celebrate their successes and learn from their failures. They don't give up or quit, but they persist and improve. Taking action and learning from feedback will help you achieve your goals and grow as an entrepreneur.

One example of a risk taker is **Sara Blakely.** She is the founder of Spanx, a company that sells shapewear for women. She is also one of the richest women in the world.

How did she become so successful? By being a risk taker.

She started Spanx in 1998 with $5,000 in savings. She had no experience in fashion or business. She had an idea to create a product that would smooth out panty lines under tight clothes.

She did her research and found out that there was no such product in the market. She also found out that most women were unhappy with their bodies and wanted to look slimmer.

She trusted her intuition and created her own prototype by cutting off the feet of her pantyhose. She also used her creativity to come up with a catchy name and logo for her product.

She took action and pitched her idea to various manufacturers, retailers, and media outlets. She faced many rejections and challenges along the way, but she didn't give up. She also learned from her feedback and improved her product based on customer needs.

She eventually got her product into Neiman Marcus, Oprah Winfrey's show, QVC, etc. She also got endorsements from celebrities like Jennifer Lopez, Gwyneth Paltrow, etc.

She grew her company from a one-woman operation to a global brand with over $1 billion in annual sales.

Amazing story! Go and do likewise.

Understand That Failure is Part of Success

Do you want to be a successful entrepreneur? If so, you need to understand that failure is part of success. Failure is not the end of the road, but the beginning of a new journey. Failure is not something to be ashamed of, but something to be proud of. Failure is not a sign of weakness, but a sign of strength.

Why do I say that? Because failure means that you tried something new and challenging. It means that you took a risk and learned something valuable. It means that you have an opportunity to improve and grow.

Many successful entrepreneurs have failed many times before they succeeded. They did not let failure stop them or discourage them. They used failure as a motivation and a lesson.

Here are some tips to help you deal with failure and turn it into success:

Accept failure as a normal and inevitable part of entrepreneurship.

Don't deny it or hide it. Don't blame yourself or others for it. Don't let it define you or limit you. Accept it as a fact and move on.

Analyze failure and learn from it.

Don't repeat the same mistakes or ignore the feedback. Don't dwell on the negative or the past. Don't let it affect your confidence or your vision. Analyze it objectively and learn from it.

Find the positive and the opportunity in failure.

Don't focus on the loss or the pain. Don't let it ruin your mood or your passion. Don't let it close your mind or your doors. Find the positive and the opportunity in failure.

Take action and try again.

Don't give up or quit. Don't wait for the perfect time or the perfect plan. Don't let fear or doubt stop you. Take action and try again.

One example of an entrepreneur who understood that failure is part of success is **Steve Jobs**. He is the co-founder of Apple, one of the most valuable and influential companies in the world. He is also one of the most admired and respected entrepreneurs in history.

How did he become so successful? By dealing with failure and turning it into success.

He started Apple in 1976 with his friend Steve Wozniak. They created the first personal computer, the Apple I, and later the Apple II, which became very popular and profitable.

But he also faced many failures along the way. He was fired from Apple in 1985 after a power struggle with the board of directors. He started another company, NeXT, which failed to sell its computers to the mass market. He also bought another company, Pixar, which struggled to make money with its animated movies.

He did not let these failures stop him or discourage him. He accepted them as part of his journey and learned from them. He found the positive and the opportunity in them.

He returned to Apple in 1997 after Apple bought NeXT for its software technology. He used his experience and vision to revitalize Apple and create new products, such as the iMac, iPod, iPhone, iPad, etc., which became very successful and changed the world.

He also turned Pixar into a successful movie studio after partnering with Disney and producing hits like Toy Story, Finding Nemo, The Incredibles, etc.

He took action and tried again until he achieved his goals and fulfilled his potential.

Never allow failure to keep you down. Shake it off and keep going!

Planner

Do you want to be your own boss and have more freedom in your life? Do you want to turn your passion into a profitable business? If so, you need to be a planner.

A planner is an entrepreneur who knows what they want and how to get it. They have a clear vision and a set of goals for their business. They also have a strategy and a plan to achieve them.

Planning is not boring or hard. It's exciting and easy if you know how to do it right. Here are some tips to help you plan your entrepreneurial journey: -

Start with your why.

Why do you want to be an entrepreneur? What is your purpose and your passion? What problem do you want to solve or what value do you want to create? Your why will give you the motivation and the direction for your business.

Define your what.

What do you want to achieve with your business? What are your short-term and long-term goals? What are your success criteria and your key performance indicators? Your what will give you the focus and the measurement for your business.

Design your how.

How do you plan to achieve your goals? What are the steps and the actions that you need to take? What are the resources and the tools that you need to use? Your how will give you the roadmap and the execution for your business.

Review and adjust.

How do you know if your plan is working or not? How do you deal with changes and challenges along the way? How do you improve and optimize your plan as you go? Reviewing and adjusting will give you the feedback and the learning for your business.

———

One example of a planner is **Mark Zuckerberg.** He is the founder of Facebook, one of the largest and most popular social media platforms in the world. He is also one of the youngest billionaires in history.

How did he become so successful? By planning his entrepreneurial journey.

He started Facebook in 2004 as a college student at Harvard. He had a vision to connect people around the world through a social network. He had a goal to reach millions of users and make money from advertising.

He designed his strategy and his plan to achieve his goal. He built his product, his team, his network, his brand, etc. He also faced many obstacles and competitors along the way, but he didn't give up.

He reviewed and adjusted his plan as he grew his business. He added new features, acquired new companies, entered new markets, etc. He also learned from his mistakes, feedback, and data.

He followed his plan until he achieved his vision and beyond.

The clock is ticking. Start planning today.

Fully Determined

Fully determined means that you are committed and focused on your goals and plans. It means that you don't give up or quit when things get hard or challenging. It means that you work hard and smart to make your business grow and succeed.

Being fully determined is not easy. You will face many obstacles and difficulties along the way. You will have to deal with a lot of work and responsibility. You will have to make tough decisions and sacrifices. You will have to learn from your failures and mistakes.

But being fully determined is also rewarding. You will be able to achieve your dreams and vision. You will be able to create value and impact for your customers and society. You will be able to enjoy the satisfaction and fulfillment of your work.

So how can you become fully determined? Here are some tips to help you: -

Have a clear and compelling vision.

A vision is a picture of what you want your business to be and do in the future. It is your purpose and your passion. It is what drives you and inspires you. Have a clear and compelling vision that motivates you every day.

Set realistic and specific goals.

Goals are the steps that you need to take to achieve your vision. They are the milestones that you need to reach and measure. They are the results that you need to deliver and celebrate. Set realistic and specific goals that challenge you and guide you.

Make a detailed and flexible plan.

A plan is a strategy that you need to follow to achieve your goals. It is the actions that you need to take and the resources that you need to use. It is the timeline that you need to follow and the contingencies that you need to prepare for. Make a detailed and flexible plan that helps you execute and adapt.

Take consistent and persistent action.

Action is the key that unlocks your potential and your success. It is the work that you need to do and the value that you need to create. It is the feedback that you need to get and the improvement that you need to make. Take consistent and persistent action that moves you forward and upward.

One example of an entrepreneur who was fully determined is **Oprah Winfrey.** She is the founder of Harpo Productions, a media company that produces TV shows, movies, magazines, books, etc. She is also one of the most influential and wealthy women in the world.

How did she become so successful? By being fully determined.

She started her career as a TV anchor in 1976. She had a vision to become a talk show host who could inspire and empower people with her stories and interviews.

She set her goals and worked hard to achieve them. She moved from one TV station to another, gaining more experience and popularity.

She made her plan and followed it with flexibility. She launched her own talk show, The Oprah Winfrey Show, in 1986, which became a huge hit and ran for 25 years.

She took action every day and never gave up on her vision. She faced many challenges, such as racism, sexism, abuse, criticism, etc., but she overcame them with courage and grace.

She followed her plan until she achieved her vision and beyond.

Copy Genius!

Passionate

Passion is the fuel that drives commitment and determination necessary to succeed on the entrepreneurial journey. As an entrepreneur, you must appreciate what you do, and it starts with knowing why you went into the business.

Being passionate means that you love what you do and why you do it. It means that you have a mission and a purpose for your business. It means that you have a fire and a drive that keeps you going.

Being passionate is not optional. It is essential. Without passion, you will not have the commitment and the determination to succeed. You will not have the energy and the enthusiasm to work hard and smart. You will not have the joy and the satisfaction of your work.

But being passionate is not enough. You also need to show it and share it.

You need to show it to yourself and to others. You need to share it with your customers and your team.

Here are some tips to help you be passionate and show it: -

Find your why.

Why did you start your business? What is your vision and your goal? What is the problem that you want to solve or the value that you want to create? Your why is the source of your passion. Find it and remind yourself of it every day.

Do what you love and love what you do.

What are the things that you enjoy doing in your business? What are the things that you are good at and that make you happy? Do more of those things and less of the things that you don't like or that drain you. Also, learn to love the things that you have to do but don't enjoy. Find ways to make them fun or meaningful.

Express your passion in everything you do.

How do you communicate your passion to others? How do you show it in your products, your services, your marketing, your branding, etc.? Express your passion in everything you do and make it visible and contagious. Use words, images, sounds, colors, etc. that reflect your passion and attract others to it.

Inspire passion in others.

How do you spread your passion to others? How do you inspire your customers, your team, your partners, etc. to be passionate about your business and your mission? Inspire passion in others by sharing your story, your vision, your values, etc. Also, listen to their stories, their needs, their feedback, etc. and show them how much you care.

ENTREPRENEURIAL TRAITS

One example of an entrepreneur who was passionate and showed it is **Tony Hsieh.** He is the founder of Zappos, an online shoe retailer that is known for its exceptional customer service and culture. He is also one of the most generous and humble entrepreneurs in history.

How did he become so successful? By being passionate and showing it.

He started Zappos in 1999 with a vision to create a company that would deliver happiness to its customers, employees, and partners. He had a passion for shoes and customer service.

He did what he loved and loved what he did. He was involved in every aspect of his business, from product selection to customer support to employee training. He also learned to love the things that he didn't like, such as dealing with investors or suppliers.

He expressed his passion in everything he did. He used words like "wow", "fun", "adventure", etc. to describe his products and his vision. He also used images, sounds, colors, etc. that reflected his passion and attracted others to it.

He inspired passion in others. He shared his story, his vision, his values, etc. with his customers, his team, his partners, etc. He also listened to their stories, their needs, their feedback, etc. and showed them how much he cared.

He followed his passion until he achieved his vision and beyond.

The world is waiting! Let your passion shine through.

Self Discipline

One trait that is common with many successful entrepreneurs is that they are masters of self-discipline. Self-discipline is the ability to control yourself and do what you need to do, even when you don't feel like it. It is the skill that helps you stay focused, motivated, and productive, no matter what challenges or distractions you face.

Self-discipline is not something that you are born with or that you can buy. It is something that you can develop and improve with practice and persistence. Here are some tips to help you become more self-disciplined: -

Set clear and realistic goals.

Goals are the targets that you want to achieve with your business. They are the reasons why you started your business and why you keep working on it. Set clear and realistic goals that are specific, measurable, achievable, relevant, and time-bound. Write them down and review them regularly.

Make a plan and stick to it.

A plan is a strategy that shows you how to achieve your goals. It is the actions that you need to take and the resources that you need to use. Make a plan that is detailed, flexible, and prioritized. Follow your plan and don't deviate from it unless necessary.

Manage your time and energy.

Time and energy are the most valuable resources that you have as an entrepreneur. You need to use them wisely and efficiently. Manage your time and energy by creating a schedule, setting deadlines, avoiding procrastination, delegating tasks, taking breaks, etc.

Monitor your progress and results.

Progress and results are the indicators that show you how well you are doing with your business. They are the feedback that tells you what works and what doesn't. Monitor your progress and results by tracking your metrics, reviewing your data, measuring your outcomes, etc.

Reward yourself and celebrate your achievements.

Rewards and celebrations are the incentives that motivate you to keep going with your business. They are the benefits that you enjoy from your hard work and discipline. Reward yourself and celebrate your achievements by giving yourself a treat, sharing your success, expressing your gratitude, etc.

One example of an entrepreneur who had self-discipline is **Jack Ma**. He is the founder of Alibaba, one of the largest e-commerce platforms in the world. He is also one of the richest people in the world.

How did he become so successful? By having self-discipline.

ENTREPRENEURIAL TRAITS

He started Alibaba in 1999 with a vision to connect small businesses in China with customers around the world. He had a goal to create an online marketplace that would empower entrepreneurs and create jobs.

He made a plan and stuck to it. He built his team, his product, his network, his brand, etc. He also faced many obstacles and competitors along the way, but he didn't give up.

He managed his time and energy by working long hours, sleeping on the floor, traveling around the world, etc. He also balanced his work with his family, his hobbies, his health, etc.

He monitored his progress and results by using data, feedback, customer satisfaction, etc. He also improved his product and service based on market needs and trends.

He rewarded himself and celebrated his achievements by donating to charity, mentoring young entrepreneurs, enjoying life, etc.

You have the potential, unleash it now.

Highly Confident

If you want to be a successful entrepreneur, you need to have high confidence. High confidence means that you believe in yourself and your abilities. It means that you can face any challenge and overcome any obstacle. It means that you can see opportunities where others see problems and risks.

High confidence is not something that you can fake or force. It is something that you can build and boost with practice and experience. Here are some tips to help you become more confident: -

Know your strengths and value.

What are the things that you are good at and that make you unique? What are the benefits and value that you can offer to your customers and partners? Know your strengths and value and use them to your advantage. Don't compare yourself to others or put yourself down. Be proud of who you are and what you can do.

Set realistic and challenging goals.

What are the things that you want to achieve with your business? What are the milestones that you want to reach and measure? Set realistic and challenging goals that are specific, measurable, achievable, relevant, and time-bound. Write them down and review them regularly.

Take action and learn from feedback.

How do you turn your goals into reality? How do you test your ideas and products in the market? Take action and don't let fear or doubt stop you. Learn from your feedback, whether positive or negative. Celebrate your successes and learn from your failures. Don't give up or quit but persist and improve.

Surround yourself with positive and supportive people.

Who are the people that inspire you and encourage you? Who are the people that share your vision and values? Surround yourself with positive and supportive people, such as mentors, coaches, peers, friends, family, etc. Listen to their advice, feedback, and encouragement. Also, give back to them by helping them with their goals and challenges.

One example of an entrepreneur who had high confidence is **Brian Chesky**. He is the co-founder of Airbnb, a platform that allows people to rent out their homes or rooms to travelers. He is also one of the most innovative and visionary entrepreneurs in history.

How did he become so successful? By having high confidence.

He started Airbnb in 2008 with his friends Joe Gebbia and Nathan

Blecharczyk. He had a vision to create a global community where people could belong anywhere. He had a passion for travel and hospitality.

He knew his strengths and value. He was good at design and storytelling. He also knew that his product would solve a problem for many people who wanted to find affordable and authentic accommodation.

He set realistic and challenging goals. He wanted to get his product into major cities around the world. He also wanted to create a brand that would stand for trust, quality, and diversity.

He took action and learned from feedback. He launched his product with a simple website that offered air mattresses in his apartment. He faced many challenges and rejections along the way, but he didn't give up. He also learned from his feedback and improved his product based on customer needs.

He surrounded himself with positive and supportive people. He got help from his friends, family, mentors, etc. He also got funding from investors like Y Combinator, Sequoia Capital, etc.

He maintained high confidence until he achieved his vision and beyond.

The future is yours, make it happen.

Highly Adaptable

One of the most important skills that you need to have as an entrepreneur is adaptability. Adaptability means that you can change and adjust to different situations and circumstances. It means that you can cope and respond quickly to any challenges or opportunities that come your way. It means that you can thrive and survive in any environment that your business faces.

Adaptability is not something that you can ignore or avoid. It is something that you need to embrace and practice. Here are some tips to help you become more adaptable: -

Be open and curious.

Don't be afraid or resistant to change. Don't be stuck or rigid in your ways. Be open and curious about new things, new ideas, new trends, new markets, etc. Learn from them and use them to your advantage.

Be flexible and creative.

Don't be limited or constrained by your plans or strategies. Don't be blind or deaf to feedback or data. Be flexible and creative in your actions and decisions. Experiment with different options and solutions. Pivot when necessary and optimize when possible.

Be resilient and optimistic.

Don't be discouraged or defeated by failures or setbacks. Don't be negative or pessimistic about the future. Be resilient and optimistic in your attitude and mindset. Bounce back from difficulties and learn from mistakes. Look for opportunities and possibilities in every situation.

Be proactive and agile.

Don't be reactive or passive to the changes around you. Don't be slow or complacent in your movements. Be proactive and agile in your approach and execution. Anticipate the changes and prepare for them. Act fast and smart to seize them.

One example of an entrepreneur who was adaptable is **Reed Hastings**. He is the co-founder of Netflix, a streaming service that offers movies, TV shows, documentaries, etc. He is also one of the most innovative and visionary entrepreneurs in history.

How did he become so successful? By being adaptable.

He started Netflix in 1997 as a DVD rental service that delivered discs by mail. He had a vision to create a convenient and affordable way for people to watch movies at home.

He was open and curious about new technologies and customer preferences. He saw the potential of streaming video over the internet and the demand for online entertainment.

He was flexible and creative in his business model and product development. He experimented with different pricing plans, subscription models, content offerings, etc. He pivoted from DVD rental to streaming service to content production.

He was resilient and optimistic in his challenges and opportunities. He faced many competitors, such as Blockbuster, Amazon, Hulu, etc., but he didn't give up. He also faced many risks, such as losing money, losing licenses, losing customers, etc., but he didn't lose hope.

He was proactive and agile in his strategy and growth. He anticipated the changes in the market and the industry and prepared for them. He acted fast and smart to capture them.

Don't hesitate, take action now and adapt where necessary.

Expert Networker

One of the most important skills that you need to have as an entrepreneur is networking. Networking means that you connect and communicate with other people who can help you and your business. It means that you build and maintain relationships that are valuable and meaningful. It means that you create and explore opportunities that are mutually beneficial.

Networking is not something that you can do once or occasionally. It is something that you need to do regularly and consistently. Here are some tips to help you become an expert networker: -

Know your purpose and goals.

Why do you want to network? What are you looking for and what can you offer? Who are the people that you want to meet and why? Know your purpose and goals and use them to guide your networking activities.

Don't network randomly or aimlessly, but strategically and intentionally.

Be proactive and outgoing.

How do you find and reach out to the people that you want to network with? How do you initiate and sustain conversations with them? Be proactive and outgoing in your networking efforts. Don't wait for people to come to you or for opportunities to fall on your lap, but go after them and create them. Use various channels and platforms, such as events, social media, email, phone, etc., to connect and communicate with your potential contacts.

Be genuine and helpful.

How do you build trust and rapport with the people that you network with? How do you add value and make a difference for them? Be genuine and helpful in your networking interactions. Don't be fake or selfish but be real and generous. Show interest and curiosity in the people that you meet, listen to their stories, needs, challenges, etc., and offer your help, advice, support, etc.

Be consistent and follow up.

How do you maintain and strengthen the relationships that you have built with the people that you network with? How do you keep in touch and stay on their radar? Be consistent and follow up with your contacts. Don't let them forget about you or lose interest in you, but remind them of your presence and value. Use various methods and occasions, such as thank-you notes, feedback requests, updates, referrals, etc., to reconnect and communicate with your contacts.

One example of an entrepreneur who was an expert networker is **Reid Hoffman**. He is the co-founder of LinkedIn, a professional networking platform that connects millions of people around the world. He is also one of the most influential and connected entrepreneurs in history.

How did he become so successful? By being an expert networker.

He started LinkedIn in 2003 with a vision to create a platform that would enable people to build their professional identity, network, and career online.

He knew his purpose and goals. He wanted to network with people who could help him grow his platform, such as investors, partners, customers, etc. He also wanted to help people network with each other and find opportunities for their careers.

He was proactive and outgoing. He used his existing connections, such as his friends from PayPal, Stanford, etc., to find and reach out to potential contacts. He also attended various events, such as conferences, meetups, etc., to meet new people and start conversations with them.

He was genuine and helpful. He built trust and rapport with the people that he networked with by being honest, friendly, curious, etc. He also added value and made a difference for them by offering his insights, introductions, endorsements, etc.

He was consistent and follow up. He maintained and strengthened the relationships that he had built with the people that he networked with by keeping in touch with them regularly. He also used his platform, LinkedIn, to reconnect and communicate with his contacts.

He used his networking skills to achieve his vision and more.

So don't wait any longer. Network your way to entrepreneurial success.

Good at Sales and Marketing

One of the most important skills that you need to have as an entrepreneur is sales and marketing. Sales and marketing mean that you know how to promote and sell your products or services to your customers. It means that you know how to communicate and persuade your customers to buy from you. It means that you know how to make money and grow your business.

Sales and marketing is not something that you can learn overnight or outsource to someone else. It is something that you need to practice and master yourself. Here are some tips to help you become good at sales and marketing: -

Know your product and your market.

What are the features and benefits of your product or service? What are the problems and needs of your customers? Know your product and your market and use them to create your unique selling proposition. Your unique selling proposition is what makes your product or service different and better than your competitors.

Know your customer and your message.

Who is your ideal customer and what are their characteristics, preferences, behaviors, etc.? What is the message that you want to convey to your customer and what are the emotions that you want to trigger in them? Know your customer and your message and use them to create your marketing strategy. Your marketing strategy is how you reach, attract, and engage your customer with your message.

Know your channels and your tools.

How do you deliver your message to your customer and where do you find them? What are the channels and tools that you use to communicate and interact with your customer? Know your channels and tools and use them to create your marketing mix. Your marketing mix is the combination of channels and tools that you use to optimize your marketing results.

Know your numbers and your goals.

How do you measure the effectiveness of your sales and marketing efforts? What are the numbers and metrics that you track and analyze? What are the goals that you set and achieve? Know your numbers and goals and use them to create your sales funnel. Your sales funnel is the process that leads your customer from awareness to purchase.

One example of an entrepreneur who was good at sales and marketing is **Richard Branson**. He is the founder of Virgin Group, a conglomerate of companies that span various industries, such as music, travel, media, etc. He is also one of the most adventurous and charismatic entrepreneurs in history.

How did he become so successful? By being good at sales and marketing.

He started his first business, a magazine called Student, in 1966 when he was 16 years old. He had a passion for journalism and activism. He wanted to create a magazine that would voice the opinions of young people.

He knew his product and his market. He knew that his magazine had unique features, such as interviews with celebrities, politicians, etc., and benefits, such as providing information, entertainment, etc., for his readers. He also knew that his market was young people who had problems, such as lack of representation, education, etc., and needs, such as expression, inspiration, etc.

He knew his customer and his message. He knew that his ideal customer was a student who was interested in current affairs, culture, etc., and who had characteristics, such as rebellious, curious, etc., preferences, such as cheap, trendy, etc., behaviors, such as reading, socializing, etc. He also knew that his message was to empower young people to make a difference in the world and that he wanted to trigger emotions, such as excitement, curiosity, etc., in them.

He knew his channels and his tools. He knew how to deliver his message to his customer and where to find them. He used various channels and tools, such as print, radio, TV, etc., to communicate and promote his magazine. He also used word-of-mouth, events, partnerships, etc., to reach and attract more customers.

He knew his numbers and his goals. He knew how to measure the effectiveness of his sales and marketing efforts. He tracked and analyzed numbers and metrics, such as circulation, revenue, costs, etc. He also set and achieved goals, such as increasing sales, expanding distribution, growing audience, etc.

He used his sales and marketing skills to grow his magazine and his business empire. He later launched other businesses, such as Virgin Records, Virgin Atlantic, Virgin Galactic, etc., using the same skills and principles.

He maximized his sales and marketing skills until he achieved his vision and beyond.

Grow your sales and marketing skills. It will pay off big time.

Manage Fear

One of the most important skills that you need to have as an entrepreneur is managing fear. Managing fear means that you can face and overcome the fears that come with starting and running a business. It means that you can use fear as a motivator and not as a barrier. It means that you can control your emotions and actions in any situation.

Managing fear is not something that you can do without or ignore. It is something that you need to do with or embrace. Here are some tips to help you manage fear: -

Identify and understand your fears.

What are the things that scare you or make you anxious about your business? What are the worst-case scenarios that you imagine or worry about? Identify and understand your fears and write them down. Don't deny or avoid them but acknowledge and accept them.

Challenge and reframe your fears.

How realistic and rational are your fears? How likely and probable are they to happen? How can you prevent or minimize them? Challenge and reframe your fears and look at them from a different perspective. Don't exaggerate or magnify them, but question and reduce them.

Take action and face your fears.

What are the steps that you need to take to overcome your fears? What are the resources that you need to use or acquire? What are the results that you expect or hope for? Take action and face your fears and don't let them stop you. Don't freeze or flee, but move and fight.

Learn from your failures and successes.

How did you deal with your fears in the past? What did you learn from your failures and successes? How can you apply those lessons to your present and future situations? Learn from your failures and successes and use them to improve your skills and confidence. Don't regret or dwell but reflect and grow.

One example of an entrepreneur who managed fear is **J.K. Rowling**. She is the author of Harry Potter, one of the most popular and successful book series in the world. She is also one of the richest and most influential women in history.

How did she become so successful? By managing fear.

She started writing Harry Potter in 1990 as a single mother living on welfare. She had a passion for writing and storytelling. She wanted to create a fantasy world that would inspire and entertain children and adults.

She identified and understood her fears. She was afraid of being poor, being rejected, being criticized, etc. She wrote down her fears and faced them.

She challenged and reframed her fears. She realized that her fears were not realistic or rational. She knew that she had nothing to lose and everything to gain by pursuing her dream. She also knew that she had the talent and the determination to succeed.

She took action and faced her fears. She finished writing her first book in 1995 and sent it to several publishers. She faced many rejections and challenges along the way, but she didn't give up. She also got feedback and support from her friends, family, agents, etc.

She learned from her failures and successes. She learned how to improve her writing, how to market her book, how to deal with fame, etc. She also applied those lessons to her subsequent books, which became bestsellers worldwide.

When fear knocks, open the door, stand tall and face it squarely.

Rule Breaker

If you want to be a successful entrepreneur, you need to be a rule breaker. Rule breaker means that you can challenge and change the status quo. It means that you can bring a different and better solution to the problems that users face. It means that you can do things that others don't dare or don't think of.

Rule breaker is not something that you can be by following or copying others. It is something that you can be by being yourself and being creative. Here are some tips to help you become a rule breaker: -

Be curious and adventurous.

Don't be satisfied or comfortable with the way things are. Don't be afraid or reluctant to try new things. Be curious and adventurous about the world and the possibilities. Explore, experiment, and discover new ideas, new markets, new products, etc.

Be bold and daring.

Don't be timid or cautious about your vision and your goals. Don't be shy or humble about your skills and your value. Be bold and daring in your actions and your decisions. Take risks, make mistakes, learn from them, and move on.

Be smart and savvy.

Don't be ignorant or naive about your industry and your competition. Don't be foolish or reckless about your resources and your opportunities. Be smart and savvy in your knowledge and your strategy. Learn from the best, leverage your strengths, optimize your results.

Be different and better.

Don't be ordinary or mediocre in your product and your service. Don't be similar or inferior to your competitors. Be different and better in your solution and your value proposition. Create something that is unique, innovative, useful, and desirable.

One example of an entrepreneur who was a rule breaker is **Mark Cuban.** He is the owner of the Dallas Mavericks, a co-founder of Broadcast.com, a star of Shark Tank, and many other ventures. He is also one of the most successful and outspoken entrepreneurs in history.

How did he become so successful? By being a rule breaker.

He started his first business, MicroSolutions, in 1983 as a software reseller. He had a passion for technology and business. He wanted to create a company that would provide high-quality and customized solutions for his clients.

ENTREPRENEURIAL TRAITS

He was curious and adventurous about the emerging technologies and trends. He explored, experimented, and discovered new ways to use computers, networks, software, etc.

He was bold and daring in his vision and his goals. He took risks, made mistakes, learned from them, and moved on. He also used his skills and his value to attract and retain customers and employees.

He was smart and savvy in his industry and his competition. He learned from the best, leveraged his strengths, optimized his results. He also used his knowledge and his strategy to grow his company and sell it for $6 million in 1990.

He was different and better in his product and his service. He created something that was unique, innovative, useful, and desirable for his clients. He also provided exceptional customer service and support.

He used his rule breaking skills to start and grow other businesses, such as Broadcast.com, HDNet, Dallas Mavericks, etc., using the same skills and principles.

Don't hold back! Break some rules.

Team Player

If you want to be a successful entrepreneur, you need to be a team player. Team player means that you can work well with other people who share your vision and goals. It means that you can collaborate, communicate, and cooperate with your team members. It means that you can leverage the skills, talents, and strengths of your team to achieve more than you could alone.

Team player is not something that you can be by isolating or dominating others. It is something that you can be by involving and empowering others. Here are some tips to help you become a team player: -

Build a diverse and complementary team.

Who are the people that you need to have on your team? What are the skills, talents, and strengths that they have or need to have? Build a diverse and complementary team that can cover all the aspects of your business, such as product, marketing, sales, finance, etc. Don't hire or partner with people who are exactly like you or who agree with everything you say, but with people who can bring different perspectives and value to your business.

Establish a clear and shared vision and goals.

What is the vision and the mission of your business? What are the goals and the objectives that you want to achieve with your business? Establish a clear and shared vision and goals for your team and communicate them clearly and frequently. Don't assume or impose your vision and goals on your team but involve them in creating and refining them.

Foster a culture of trust and respect.

How do you treat and interact with your team members? How do you create a positive and productive work environment for your team? Foster a culture of trust and respect for your team and show it in your actions and words. Don't micromanage or criticize your team members, but trust and support them. Don't blame or judge your team members but appreciate and recognize them.

Encourage collaboration and communication.

How do you share information and ideas with your team members? How do you solicit feedback and input from your team members? Encourage collaboration and communication among your team and facilitate it with tools and methods. Don't hoard or hide information or ideas from your team but share and exchange them. Don't ignore or dismiss feedback or input from your team but listen and consider them.

One example of an entrepreneur who was a team player is **Arianna**

Huffington. She is the co-founder of The Huffington Post, a news and opinion website that became one of the most popular and influential media outlets in the world. She is also the founder of Thrive Global, a company that promotes well-being and productivity.

How did she become so successful? By being a team player.

She started The Huffington Post in 2005 with her partners Kenneth Lerer, Jonah Peretti, and Andrew Breitbart. She had a vision to create a platform that would offer news, commentary, blogs, etc., from various sources and perspectives.

She built a diverse and complementary team that had skills, talents, and strengths in journalism, technology, business, etc. She also hired or partnered with people who had different opinions and backgrounds from her own.

She established a clear and shared vision and goals for her team and communicated them clearly and frequently. She involved her team in creating and refining the vision and goals of the platform.

She fostered a culture of trust and respect for her team and showed it in her actions and words. She trusted and supported her team members in their work and gave them autonomy and responsibility. She also appreciated and recognized their contributions and achievements.

She encouraged collaboration and communication among her team and facilitated it with tools and methods. She shared and exchanged information and ideas with her team members and solicited feedback and input from them. She also listened and considered their feedback and input and made changes accordingly.

She used her team player skills to grow her platform and her business empire. She later launched other businesses, such as Thrive Global, using the same skills and principles.

Don't wait any longer. Become a team player today and start building your highly successful business!

64

Conclusion

You have just read about the traits of successful entrepreneurs. You might be wondering if you have what it takes to be one of them. You might be curious to know how you can develop and apply those traits to your own business ideas.

The good news is that you don't have to be born with those traits. You can learn and practice them with time and effort. The bad news is that you can't just read about them and expect to become a successful entrepreneur. You must take action and start building your business.

Successful entrepreneurs are not just dreamers, they are doers. They don't just think about their ideas, they test them in the market. They don't just plan their strategies; they execute them in the field. They don't just wait for opportunities, they create them.

Here are some practical steps that you can take to become a successful entrepreneur: -

Start with a problem and a solution.

What is a problem that you or someone else faces? What is a solution that you can offer to solve that problem? Start with a problem and a solution that you are passionate about and that you have some knowledge or experience in.

Validate your idea and your market.

How do you know if your solution is viable and desirable? How do you know if there is a market for your solution? Validate your idea and your market by doing some research, talking to potential customers, getting feedback, etc.

Build a minimum viable product and a value proposition.

What is the simplest version of your solution that you can build and offer to your customers? What is the benefit and value that your solution provides to your customers? Build a minimum viable product and a value proposition that you can test and improve with your customers.

Find your customer and your message.

Who is your ideal customer and what are their characteristics, preferences, behaviors, etc.? What is the message that you want to convey to your customer and what are the emotions that you want to trigger in them? Find your customer and your message and use them to create your marketing strategy.

Scale your product and your business. How do you grow your product and your customer base? How do you optimize your product and your customer satisfaction? How do you generate revenue and profit from your product and your business? Scale your product and your business by using various tools and methods, such as growth hacking, business models, etc.

———

One example of an entrepreneur who followed these steps is **Drew Houston**. He is the co-founder of Dropbox, a cloud storage service that allows users to store and share files online. He is also one of the youngest billionaires in the world.

How did he become so successful? By following these steps.

He started Dropbox in 2007 with a problem and a solution. He had a problem of forgetting his USB drive at home or losing it. He had a solution of creating a service that would sync his files across his devices and the internet.

He validated his idea and his market by doing some research, talking to potential customers, getting feedback, etc. He found out that there was a demand for his solution and that there was no existing service that offered what he wanted.

He built a minimum viable product and a value proposition that he could test and improve with his customers. He built a simple prototype of his service that allowed users to upload, download, and sync files online. He also created a video that showed the benefit and value of his service to his customers.

He found his customer and his message and used them to create his marketing strategy. He knew that his ideal customer was someone who needed to access their files from anywhere and anytime. He also knew that his message was to make life easier for his customers by saving them time, space, and hassle. He used various channels and tools, such as blogs, forums, referrals, etc., to reach, attract, and engage his customers with his message.

He scaled his product and his business by using various tools and methods, such as growth hacking, business models, etc. He used various techniques, such as viral marketing, freemium model, partnerships, etc., to grow his product and his customer base.

He also optimized his product and his customer satisfaction by adding new features, improving performance, offering support, etc. He also generated revenue and profit from his product and his business by charging for premium plans, advertising, etc.

He followed these steps until he achieved his vision and beyond.

Many things are possible on the entrepreneurial journey. So don't wait any longer. Start taking action today and start developing this traits. I look forward to celebrating your entrepreneurial success very soon.

To Your Massive Success,

OG Arizechi

Also by OG Arizechi

Entrepreneurial Traits

Watch for more at https://www.kapublishing.com.

About the Author

Meet OG Arizechi, the unstoppable force behind KA Publishing, a powerhouse in the world of written wisdom. With a sharp entrepreneurial mind and a penchant for publishing, OG has orchestrated the creation of numerous impactful books and resources. These literary treasures delve into the realms of Internet Marketing, Online Business Strategies, Profitable Ventures, and the intricacies of Artificial Intelligence.

But OG's influence doesn't stop there. He's the visionary founder of KA Digest, a platform that once was KonnectAfrica.Net, now a pulsating hub of inspiration. Dubbed Africa's Premier Inspirational Platform, KA Digest shines the spotlight on African Super Achievers. Through riveting profiles, insightful interviews, and compelling features, OG ignites the flames of Entrepreneurship, fuels the engines of Career Development, and powers the gears of Employment across Africa.

Behind OG's success lies a rock-solid foundation of financial acumen and a mastery of data. As a Chartered Accountant and seasoned Data Scientist, he possesses a wealth of knowledge gleaned from over a decade of navigating the complex structures of multinational corporations. He understands the DNA of highly profitable businesses, unraveling their secrets with precision.

Driven by an unwavering passion for the African Continent's rapid ascent, OG is on a mission. His fervor lies in inspiring the youth, not just in Africa, but globally, urging them to awaken, chase their dreams, and unleash their full potential upon the world.

OG isn't just an advocate; he's a zealous crusader, waving the banner of possibility high above Africa's fertile soil. His motivation knows no bounds, propelling him to shape a better world for us all.

Read more at https://www.kapublishing.com.

About the Publisher

KA Publishing is a leading provider of resources, books, courses, and trainings for individuals and businesses who seek to grow and develop in the areas of internet marketing and online business, inspiration and motivation, book summaries, and education. We are committed to providing high-quality, informative content that inspires, educates, and empowers our readers to achieve their personal, professional and corporate goals.

Read more at https://kapublishing.com/.